Luc et Sophie

# French Stories for Primary School Pupils, Level 1

## 7 Specially Written Short Stories for Beginning Learners

Barbara Scanes

For instructions on how to download your free audio files and printable resources for the stories, please see page 57.

**Brilliant**
PUBLICATIONS

# Contents

**Downloadable files**

The downloadable files include an audio recording of the story and vocabulary list for each story (eg. LSF1-1-STORY-AUDIO.mp3 and LSF1-1-VOCAB-AUDIO.mp3) as well as a pdf file containing the English translations for all 7 stories (LSF1-TRANSLATIONS-PDF.pdf)

Published by Brilliant Publications Limited, Unit 10, Sparrow Hall Farm, Edlesborough, Dunstable, LU6 2ES.
www.brilliantpublications.co.uk
The name 'Brilliant Publications' is a registered trade mark.

Written by Barbara Scanes
Illustrated by Paul Hutchinson
© Barbara Scanes and Brilliant Publications Limited 2014
ISBN printed book: 978-1-78317-382-2
ISBN PDF book:    978-1-78317-386-0

First printed and published in the UK as 7 individual books in 2014. First printed and published in this collection in 2024.

The right of Barbara Scanes to be identified as the author of this work has been asserted by herself in accordance with the Copyright, Designs and Patents Act 1988.

# Bonjour

2

5

**Non ! C'est moi, maman.**

**Alors levez-vous, s'il vous plaît !**

7

# Vocabulaire

| | |
|---|---|
| bonjour | good morning/hello |
| écoutez | listen |
| levez-vous | get up |
| regardez | look |
| un crocodile | a crocodile |
| non | no |
| c'est moi | it's me |
| maman | mum |
| alors | so |
| s'il vous plaît | please |

# Je m'appelle Sophie

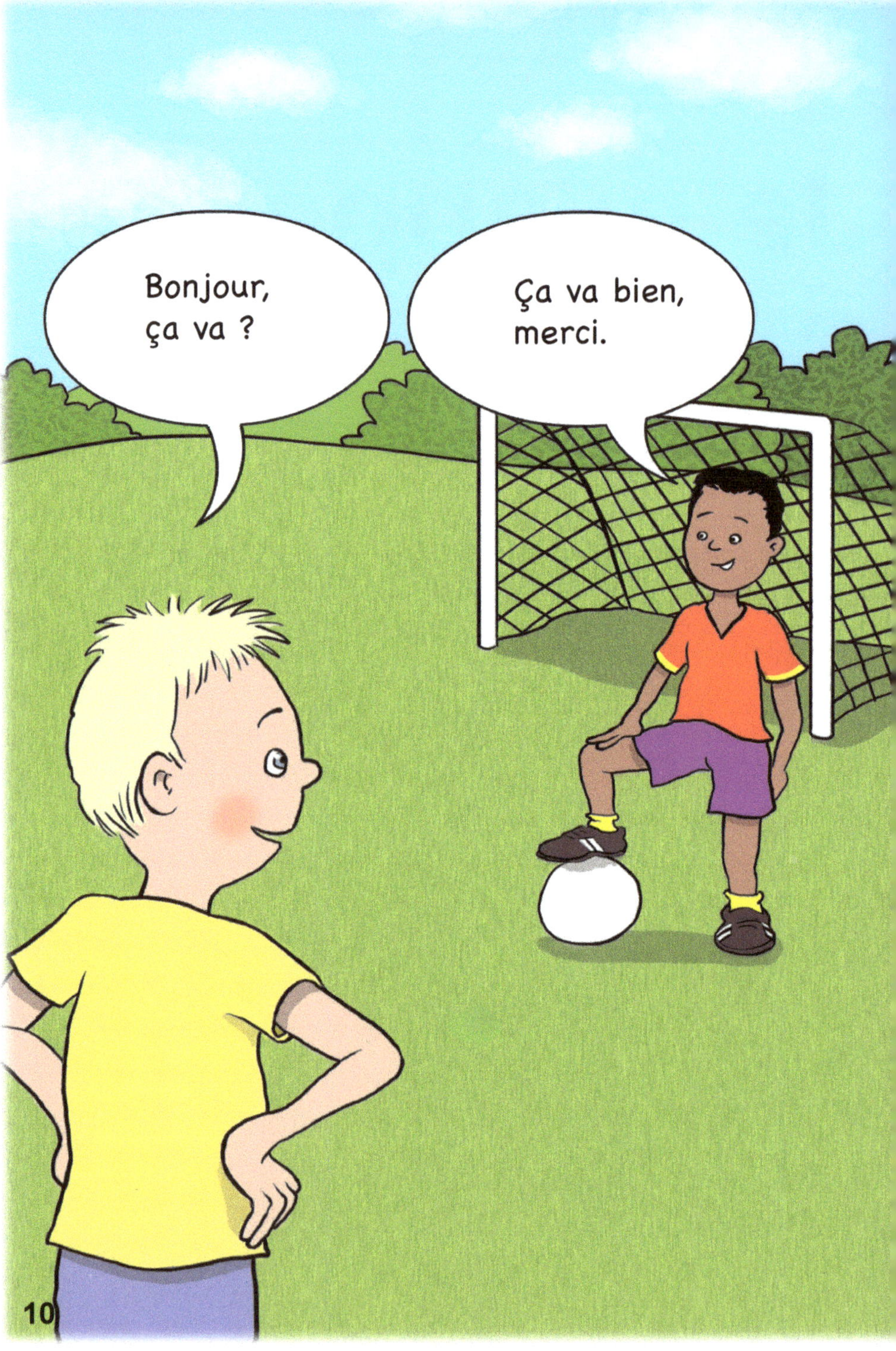
Bonjour, ça va ?
Ça va bien, merci.

11

13

Ça va ?

15

# Vocabulaire

| | |
|---|---|
| ça va ? | how are you?/are you OK?/how are things? |
| ça va | I'm fine/things are fine |
| bien | well/fine |
| ça va bien | I'm very well |
| merci | thank you |
| comment t'appelles-tu ? | what's your name? |
| je m'appelle ... | my name is... |
| et toi ? | and you? |
| ça va mal | I'm not well/things are bad |
| maman arrive | mum's coming |
| au revoir | goodbye |

# Combien de biscuits ?

19

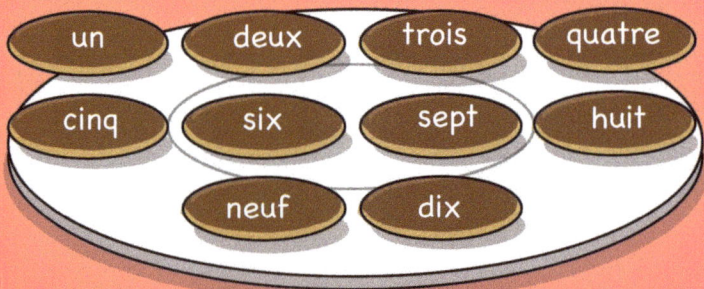

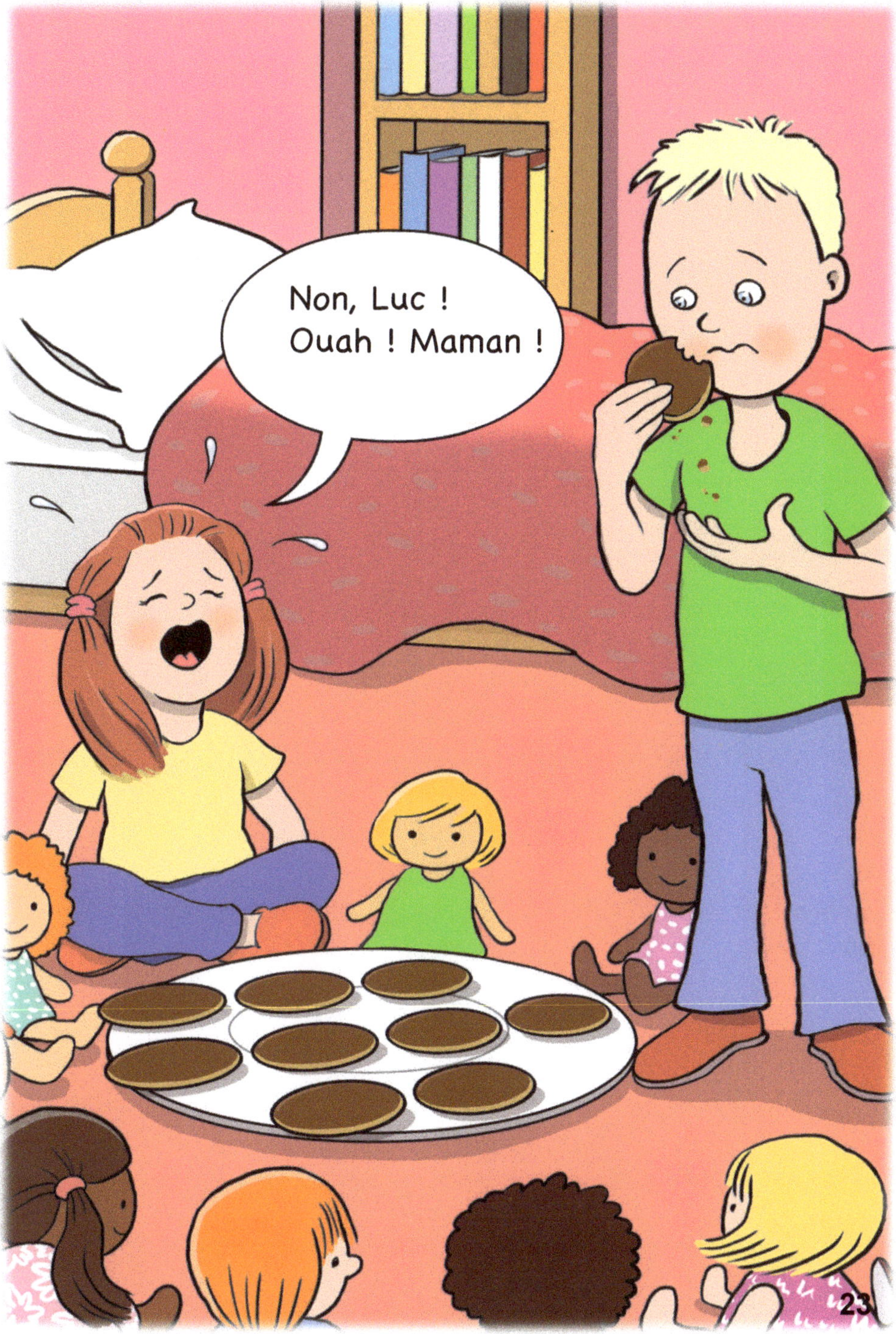
Non, Luc !
Ouah ! Maman !

# Vocabulaire

| | |
|---|---|
| combien de biscuits ? | how many biscuits? |
| j'ai | I have |
| tu as | you have |
| un biscuit | a biscuit |
| des biscuits | some biscuits |
| salut | hi (can also mean 'bye) |
| oui | yes |
| ils sont | they are |
| pour | for |
| mes poupées | my dolls |
| mais | but |
| beaucoup (de) | lots (of) |
| un | one |
| deux | two |
| trois | three |
| quatre | four |
| cinq | five |
| six | six |
| sept | seven |
| huit | eight |
| neuf | nine |
| dix | ten |
| et | and |
| combien (de) ? | how much?/how many (of)? |
| moi | me |

# J'ai six ans

J'ai six ans.
Et toi ?

J'ai cinq ans.

Moi, j'ai huit ans.

29

31

# Vocabulaire

| | |
|---|---|
| quel âge as-tu ? | how old are you? |
| j'ai six ans | I'm six (years old) |
| tu as sept ans | you're seven (years old) |
| tu as sept ans ? | are you seven (years old)? |
| c'est | it is |
| bientôt | soon |
| mon anniversaire | my birthday |
| en ce moment | at the moment |
| tu es | you are |
| un bébé | a baby |

# J'ai un frère

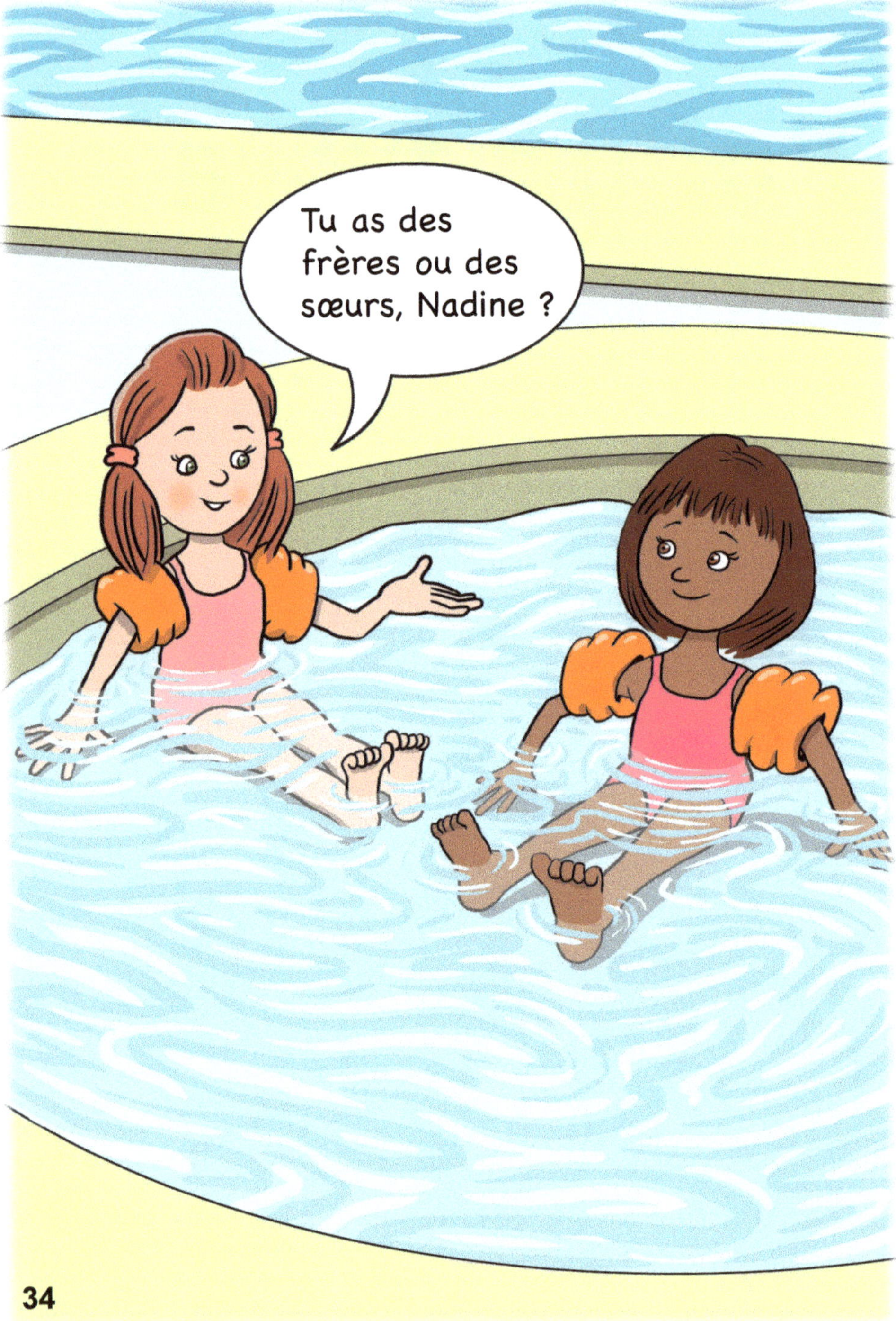
Tu as des frères ou des sœurs, Nadine ?

Oui,
j'ai deux frères et
une petite sœur.
Elle a trois ans.

Et toi ?

J'ai un frère, mais je voudrais une sœur.

37

39

# Vocabulaire

| | |
|---|---|
| tu as ? | have you (got)? |
| des frères | some brothers |
| des sœurs | some sisters |
| ou | or |
| une sœur | a sister |
| une petite sœur | a little sister |
| un frère | a brother |
| deux frères | two brothers |
| elle a trois ans | she is three (years old) |
| je voudrais | I would like |
| c'est qui ? | who is that?/who is it? |
| mon frère | my brother |
| il est | he is |
| bête | silly |
| être | to be |
| enfant unique | only child |

# Beaucoup de bonbons

Eh ! Regardez ! Sophie a des bonbons !

43

45

... onze, douze, treize, quatorze, quinze, seize, dix-sept, dix-huit, dix-neuf, vingt.

Alors, quatre bonbons pour moi, quatre pour Henri, quatre pour Luc, quatre pour Nadine et quatre pour Sophie.

Non !
Zéro bonbons pour toi,
zéro pour Henri,
zéro pour Luc,
dix pour Nadine
et dix pour moi !
Au revoir !

# Vocabulaire

| | |
|---|---|
| Sophie a | Sophie has |
| un bonbon | a sweet |
| des bonbons | some sweets |
| tu as combien de ... ? | how many ... do you have? |
| onze | eleven |
| douze | twelve |
| treize | thirteen |
| quatorze | fourteen |
| quinze | fifteen |
| seize | sixteen |
| dix-sept | seventeen |
| dix-huit | eighteen |
| dix-neuf | nineteen |
| vingt | twenty |
| zéro | zero |

# Un bonbon rouge

Alors, fermez les yeux !
Et moi, j'ai un bonbon orange,
un bonbon rose,
un bonbon violet
et un bonbon marron.

Ouvrez les yeux !
Pour gagner un
bonbon, devinez la
couleur qui manque !

53

55

# Vocabulaire

| | |
|---|---|
| seul | only/alone |
| rouge | red |
| bleu | blue |
| vert | green |
| jaune | yellow |
| orange | orange |
| rose | pink |
| violet | purple |
| marron | brown |
| fermez les yeux | close your eyes |
| ouvrez les yeux | open your eyes |
| gagner | to win |
| devinez | guess |
| la couleur | the colour |
| qui manque | which is missing |
| c'est le rouge | it's the red (one) |
| c'est nul ! | it's rubbish/that's rubbish |

# Download instructions

To download your free resources for **Luc et Sophie French Stories for Primary School Pupils, Level 1**:

Go to: **https://www.brilliantpublications.education**

You will need to set up a log in with an email address and password if you do not already have one for the https://www.brilliantpublications.education website. (Please note: you will need to set up a new account on this website to download your files, even if you already have an account on our main website.)

Your username may contain: letters, numbers and the special characters * - _ . @

You will be asked to confirm your email address by clicking the validation link emailed to you when you register.

Don't forget to check in spam/junk if you do not see an email from us.

We have introduced 2-factor authorisation on this website to make it more secure. This means that whenever you log in, you will be sent a numerical authorisation code by email which you must copy and paste into the welcome page on the website. The authentication code only lasts 1 hour.

Once logged on, choose the **French** category and click on the cover for **Luc et Sophie French Stories for Primary School Pupils, Level 1**.

Your unique password for the downloads is: **93ypR6uGB**

The downloaded filename will be **French-Stories-Level-1.zip**

Please note, the password will be changed at regular intervals so make sure you have a copy of the files once you have downloaded them.

If you experience any difficulties with downloading your files, please email info@brilliantpublications.co.uk and we will get back to you as soon as possible.

Depending on the speed of your internet and the size of the download, it may take some time for the download to complete. To avoid problems, please make sure that your computer does not go to sleep during the download.

Note: We test the software on PCs and Apple Macs, but there are too many different types of hardware in schools for us to be able to test it on every device owned by schools.

www.ingramcontent.com/pod-product-compliance
Lightning Source LLC
Chambersburg PA
CBHW050015090426
42734CB00020B/3278